Renaming the Seasons

poems by

Judy Kaber

Finishing Line Press
Georgetown, Kentucky

Renaming the Seasons

For Karie Friedman
1940 – 2017

Author's Note: In 2008. After receiving an MFA from New England College, Karie Friedman established the poetry critique group The Poets' Table, based in Belfast, Maine. I joined this group in 2009 where Karie set the tone for thoughtful and serious commenting, with an eye towards publication. We usually met in the basement of the Belfast Historical Museum surrounded by boxes containing items yet to be catalogued.

Copyright © 2019 by Judy Kaber
ISBN 978-1-63534-908-5 First Edition
All rights reserved under International and Pan-American Copyright Conventions.
No part of this book may be reproduced in any manner whatsoever without written permission from the publisher, except in the case of brief quotations embodied in critical articles and reviews.

ACKNOWLEDGMENTS

Special thanks to the editors of the following publication in which this poem first appeared:

december- "The Unsuspecting Gardener"

Publisher: Leah Maines
Editor: Christen Kincaid
Cover Art: Marjorie Arnett
Author Photo: Marjorie Arnett
Cover Design: Leah Huete

Printed in the USA on acid-free paper.
Order online: www.finishinglinepress.com
also available on amazon.com

Author inquiries and mail orders:
Finishing Line Press
P. O. Box 1626
Georgetown, Kentucky 40324
U. S. A.

Table of Contents

Cento 1

The Loyalty of Chickens 2

All That Belongs to us Is Time 3

Washing Clothes at the Laundromat 4

The Unsuspecting Gardener 5

A Change in Routine 6

Yellow Boat 8

A Scant Amount of Time 9

You Are Ashes Now 10

A Brief Elegy 11

Inside You a Door 12

Body Of Water 13

After You Leave 15

Ice 16

Grief 17

Poem in the Beginning of Spring 18

The End of a Journey 19

sunlight through an iron fence
patterns the snow so gently
it calls out to be shared

Karie Friedman

Cento
      lines from Karie Friedman's book Add Water, Add Fire

Down through a capillary system
I feel the heat and climb out of the earth,
tasting air and leaf, translucent as new stems,
steaming under April stars. I'm ready

for the sky to fall, for its voluptuous hell.
Who laid these bricks with sun—
clear, with lacy veins, a rim of tender green?
My daughters have taught me—

deep in tickseed, hawkweed, lupine,
in the field of a thousand stems:
we wander this firmament like dust motes.
I'm folded under quilts in blessed dark,

only a human heart, pumping stubbornly,
until it seems the grasses speak,
and cows wade, wet to the knees,
glowing in life's stubborn sweetness.

The Loyalty of Chickens
after William Carlos Williams

In the hospital there was so
little I could do. We didn't talk much,
kept propping each other up, *it depends*
we kept thinking, upon transfusions, upon
blood counts, when your fate was already a
signed, sealed, delivered deal, red
cells crowded out, white like a wheelbarrow
full of despair in your veins. Hope glazed
our faces, a brittle sheen with
too many cracks. We discussed rain,
wind, weather, as if the water
of the world could wash this away, while beside
the cranked-up bed, I put down the
charger you asked for, the white
comb, a book called *The Loyalty of Chickens*.

All That Belongs to Us Is Time

You were born into a usual body
muscle and limbs, tarsals, metatarsals—
with only so many ways to bend.

Eventually joints tire of this flexing,
this shifting from place to place
as if the air is full of string and you are

weaving something new. For isn't this
what you want to do? But cartilage wears
away, bones like rocks rubbing,

and pain becomes a vicious animal
digging in with claws that only you can feel.
When you kneel in the garden

the earth is no longer generous, no longer
gives as easily as it once did. When you rise,
your knees shout foul-mouthed words.

Some days you drink a tonic, a concoction
of garlic, lemon, salt, trying to ward off
demons with their thorny throats

and calloused hands. It's time to harvest
parsley and mint, to hang it from strings to dry,
yet you sit at the table drinking chamomile tea

waiting for the exact moment to go outside,
just as you once sat composing, holding hands
above the keyboard anticipating the unfolding

of the poem, some soft neonate that only you
could generate, that you could lift up in tired palms,
could set breathing on the body of the world.

Washing Clothes at the Laundromat

Even though you are in pain,
you go next door to the bookstore,
talk with owner about what to order,
the cadence of your voices matching
nearby traffic, the rattle of stroller wheels outside.
Domesticity and poetry—they are the engines
that drive you through your days. Walking
with your cane to the health food store,
you nod to a man passing on a bike.

Inside the marrow of your bones,
your blood has come undone, a secret failing.
You return to dry the clothes, place filled
with the wet smack of cloth against metal,
humid air, plastic chairs aligned
beneath the window in the sun.
Quarters drop one by one in the slot.

Hot air blasts as you watch, worn
linoleum beneath your feet. So unlike
the meadow grass beneath the feet
of the woman who hung her clothes
from sagging lines in sun, a child
in her belly, all the words
of her song as yet unsung.

The Unsuspecting Gardener

It began innocently, the way most things do—
the seed planted in good ground, the ovum
splitting again and again, the first kiss
in the front seat of an aqua 1955 Chevy
station wagon, wipers thumping against rain—

when you reached too far to pull the last weed
from beneath the narcissus, its head
already dead and gone. Somehow the tilt of body
wrong, you plummeted to the brick walk.
After, you limped into the house, surveyed

the leg, which in days ahead turned purple,
blue. The cost of growing old, you thought.
An inconvenience. Nothing that stopped you
from cooking dinner, making the bed, speaking
to your daughter on the phone. And Thursday,

the day you always went into town for groceries,
laundry, a visit to the local bookstore—you did
that too. Even went out for an evening of music,
as your lower leg swelled and hurt
more than it should. How could you know

that your very bones had betrayed you—
the orderly birth of white and red cells turned
into pandemonium, a blossoming of random
blasts, good for nothing except chaos?
No lumps on your breasts

when you raised your arm, no odd-shaped
blotches on skin, no bleeding. Only a bit of tiredness,
a new drag to your step that could have been age,
that could have been anything—a virus, a slight
cold, the humid air weighing you down.

A Change in Routine

When I pull up to your house,
search in the shed for the key,
a man drives up, gets out of his car,
asks what I am looking for. Gray hair
hangs lank about his head, uncombed,
like strands of stray grass.

When I talk to him, he turns away and answers
in a voice as dry as wood shavings.
He's looking for you. I give him the short version—
how you fell while weeding flowers, your leg swelled
with so much pain you called the ambulance
and now you are in the hospital,
but they've found something else—
so there's no telling when you'll be
home again.

He shifts from leg to leg, turns
into the breeze, his words drifting like seeds
from a dandelion flower across the grass
and I come to understand that he's the one
who mows your lawn and stacks your wood.
He's come wanting money, needing to be paid
right away as is so often the case
with part-time men. In his passenger seat,
a woman sits, her face gray behind glass.

I want the man to go away so I can get
what I came for, but he goes on
talking, worried about the money. He says
you are almost always here when he comes by.
As if you are guilty for going away. As if
you have let him down and now he doesn't
know what to do.

I tell him to call the hospital and finally
he understands that this is all he can do,
that I cannot tell him when you will be back
to press a bundle of bills into his hand,
that the world has let him down on this,
as it always does, as it always will.

Yellow Boat

Although coats still hang in the entryway
and boots still line the floor ready
for the next storm, they will remain
dry even as snow covers the roads.
And soon memory swept away,
and soon heartache.

As the poets stand before the audience,
reciting their poems, your bones cry
in faded voice of cells, of sorrow.
And the door closes,
and soon heartache.

Cured and trimmed,
onions fill great baskets on the table,
teacups cleaned and placed on shelves,
crumbs brushed into a bag beneath the sink.
Always this ordering.

Pickles handed out to neighbors,
dilly beans full of vinegar and spice. So many
times you washed your hands in the sink,
labeled tablecloths, stacked boxes
in the attic.

Names that once stood for something,
now air. What could have been,
never was. I imagine you stepping
into my house, across dusty floor.
I am sorry I never held you there.

Water rises, pulls free the earth.
Too early now to plant seeds, only
to be swept away in flood. This morning
a yellow boat torn loose lodged
on the opposite shore. Whatever holds it,
may yet let go.

A Scant Amount of Time

In vain we gather round the table, take our seats,
in vain the dust turns beneath fluorescent lights,

in vain boxes on the shelves spell out the past,
our fingers bend around our pens. We yearn

to fill the emptiness with words, to conjure up
your presence in a chair. Yet you've left

your garden plants among purslane
and pigweed, your flowers thick with quackgrass

and ragweed. Garlic sprawls across
your counters, your bed remains unmade. Untended

books rise in a pile beside your chair. In vain
they wait for your hands to turn the pages, a touch

like unwashed sleep. Oh friend, how far
we've come in missing you! In vain we sketch

lyrical lines in air and call it real, we drink your tea
and taste the heather of you there.

You Are Ashes Now

and your daughter ponders whether to toss them in the compost pile or maybe underneath a plant that needs the soil more alkaline. She tells me you have not left a map of the garden and that she has been keeping a journal of her moods. Right now she is in a place where too many voices shout at her, too confused to give them names or concentrate. I am no help with the plants, these alien species pushing from earth, twining stems around thin posts so they may hang their heavy heads. And as to feelings, my own have escaped me, spilled across my desk with the other clutter tumbling across your book of poems, your voice as fresh as yesterday.

A Brief Elegy

I grieve the loss of a witness
of small things—

a slip, stained dark and torn,
uncovered beneath floorboards,

a sheet of ice cut to lace,
a gaggle of wild turkeys

descending the hill, broken
narrow-necked bottles that once held

Dr. Kilmer's Swamp Root Cure,
a mouse escaping burning brush,

a house sinking
under white waves of snow,

a glass raised to a dead lover,
a woman on a brick walk who falls

remembering
the summer day she wore a rose in her hair.

Inside You a Door

Outside only rain
swelling the stream, constant sound
of gray, an underground sadness.

I open that door and the world comes
into my kitchen. Jazzy stars
fill my breast. Remember the night

we sat at Elm Street Grill, the wheat
of our happiness threshed on the floor,
band squeezed in the corner? We watched them,

ate pizza, ignored the simple pleasure—
the in and out—of each other's breath. Until
yours vanished in a cellular haze.

I think of us running through rain
in Salem, feet soaked with poetry, windows
fogged. I could be left in that space

where nothing moves. Except
I have gone through the door of you,
picked up the poems that were

scattered everywhere, pieced them
together into a vision of possibility,
kept your voice alive, unobstructed and endless.

Body of Water

In the morning when I rise
a gray blush of ice partially drapes the stream
like a raw-boned veil. One log,
branches flung wide, head submerged,
rests in the middle, immobile.

Rocks stand capped with snow.
Banks rise—crowded with roots
fingering water, with leaves packed
in tight beds—to the lean length
of trees, to the sky overhead.
A compact sun.

Somewhere there is movement,
but not here.

In the depths, frogs continue,
hearts dragged to near standstill.
Tiny emerald scales of duckweed
shimmer in mud.

Under the ice, huddled masses
of water boatmen and backswimmers
drift in air pockets.
I wear a robe in the cold room,
move about in slippers—

to the shed to gather kindling,
to the stove to light the fire.
Summer suits me better,
the way light overflows, green
pushing its way into the house
like a handsome marauder.

It's not yet a year since your death.
I rename the seasons:

Season of False Belief.
Season of Clenched Hands.
Season of Weeping.
Season of Gray Veil.

After You Leave

Maple leaves turn red.
Yet days stay warm as if
summer forgets how
to move into autumn.

After you leave I sit
with your shadow
listening to blues.
When I read your poems,
your voice sinks into me,
like molasses into a drink
to cure my grief.

In baskets on your table
onions you dug from the earth
crowd together.
I carry some away
in a paper bag.

So many recipes need onions.
Sharp knife in my hand,
eyes tearing, I slice this bulb
pulled from tender earth.

Ice

Today I spread
coal ashes over
ice-riddled ground
step where it isn't slick
I never saw you
in the end lying
in the hospital bed
books piled like
bodies of birds unread
it's possible the end
of the driveway
remains blocked
from all the plow left
your daughters
said you didn't
suffer I wonder
if maybe one last
word one last
poem creased your lips
or filled some hollow
space in your mind's mouth
the past—bones—
glass—clear as
bare trees the way
twigs poke frozen
beside ridges
the way ground
calls out beneath
booted feet

Grief

From the window in the kitchen
I can't see the yellow paddle boat
now further down stream, stuck
among the rocks, green
just beginning to edge the banks,
water broken by the hard back
of spring, thick bubbles of white
pressing through.

In the kitchen I can't hear
the hollow thrash of water
against plastic, the clang, clang
of rudder hitting the clock
of riddled dam, the boxed
bracket of captivity.

In the kitchen I think
about windows, smudged glass,
the way the stream has carried
the yellow boat, the current

going only down, boat now
stuck, now free, now
almost through
as I watch from the kitchen.

poem in the beginning of spring

> *"a faint light*
> *gleams on their rounded shoulders*
> *after a long trip from the stars."*
> —Karie Friedman

I keep your book at hand so the sound of the day's
wakening can rise, so that I can find
warmth in words you chose, your sight fallen
on the page as surely as light falls across window ledge.
Today I will pen you into my life. Today I will rise
from my chair and carry you into the world. Your breath
        now my song, gleaming.

Car thumping down muddy road, for years
you graced the old house. How can this be gone?
Voice silk scarf, hands crafting each instant—
so much fallen in the day's leaves. Green buds
thread trees, your garden carries you heart's
leavings, echoes the grace of your touch,
        given, given, until—

birds return to feeders, in an instant
wings flicker on glass. The world rolls in change
like a wet puppy. I only wish you were
conceived as tree, rising, rising. Luminous
stars kneeling, named and nameless.
Flashlight sinking in a well, sweeping,
        a final glimmer.

Dissipated in the egg-yolk sky, high
in the plasma night, your star-sewn skin
stretches, falls again, into the earth,
into careening stream. It's you I am seeing
in owl's call, in willow bark, in seeds. No dream
woman, but real as prevailing wind, as liquescent ice,
        as my nascent thaw.

The End of a Journey

The spacecraft Cassini crashed into Saturn,
a shooting star in that planet's sky and no more measurements
streamed one billion miles back to Earth.

When I phone, your daughter answers, says you died
yesterday, my heart breaks down into strange hisses
as if all the air has gone out, as if it has burned
to sizzling ash.
                       So many images and wonders lost with you.
A core of sadness lies buried deep in shifting molecules.

Twisting, disintegrating as they fall, the casings around plutonium
are the last to go.
                       You go so quickly, body
oxygen-starved, blood cells tumbling, caught in the push
of blast cells. When they try to wake you, you press deeper
into inner space, plunge finally beyond our grasp.
                       Hundreds
of people gather for Cassini's dive, and when the signal disappears
a scientist's daughter cries and hugs her father. It's hard
          to explain, she says.

Judy Kaber was born in Brooklyn, NY, and grew up on Long Island. Graduating from high school in the sixties, she initially attended college in Buffalo, but dropped out of school before completing a semester. In 1971, she moved to Ripley, Maine, where she and her husband purchased an old house and 25 acres of land. During her time in Ripley, she grew vegetables and had numerous animals, including goats, ducks, sheep, and an Angus steer called Mr. Moose. Judy returned to college, earned a Masters in Education with a focus on teaching writing. In 1997 she became a Fellow in the Maine Writing Project. She taught elementary school for 34 years before retiring in 2014.

In high school, nurtured by Laura Langford, a talented teacher, Judy began writing poetry seriously. Since then, she has continued to develop her craft through reading, classes, workshops, and continued writing. She has been a member of the critique group, The Poet's Table, since 2009, and is also a member of the online poetry board, *The Waters*. Her poems have appeared in many journals, both print and electronic, including *Atlanta Review, december, The Guardian, Off the Coast, The Comstock Review, Tar River,* and *Spillway*. In 2009 she won the Maine Postmark Poetry Contest. Her chapbook, *Rehearsing in the Dark*, won the Larry Kramer Memorial Chapbook Contest in 2011, and in 2016 she won second place in the Muriel Kraft Bailey Poetry Contest judged by Marge Piercy.

www.ingramcontent.com/pod-product-compliance
Lightning Source LLC
LaVergne TN
LVHW041524070426
835507LV00012B/1798